HOW TO BEAT

SOCIAL ANXIETY

Step by Step and Proven Techniques for Overcoming

Anxiety and Shyness.

NOAH HOOPER

Tables Of Contents

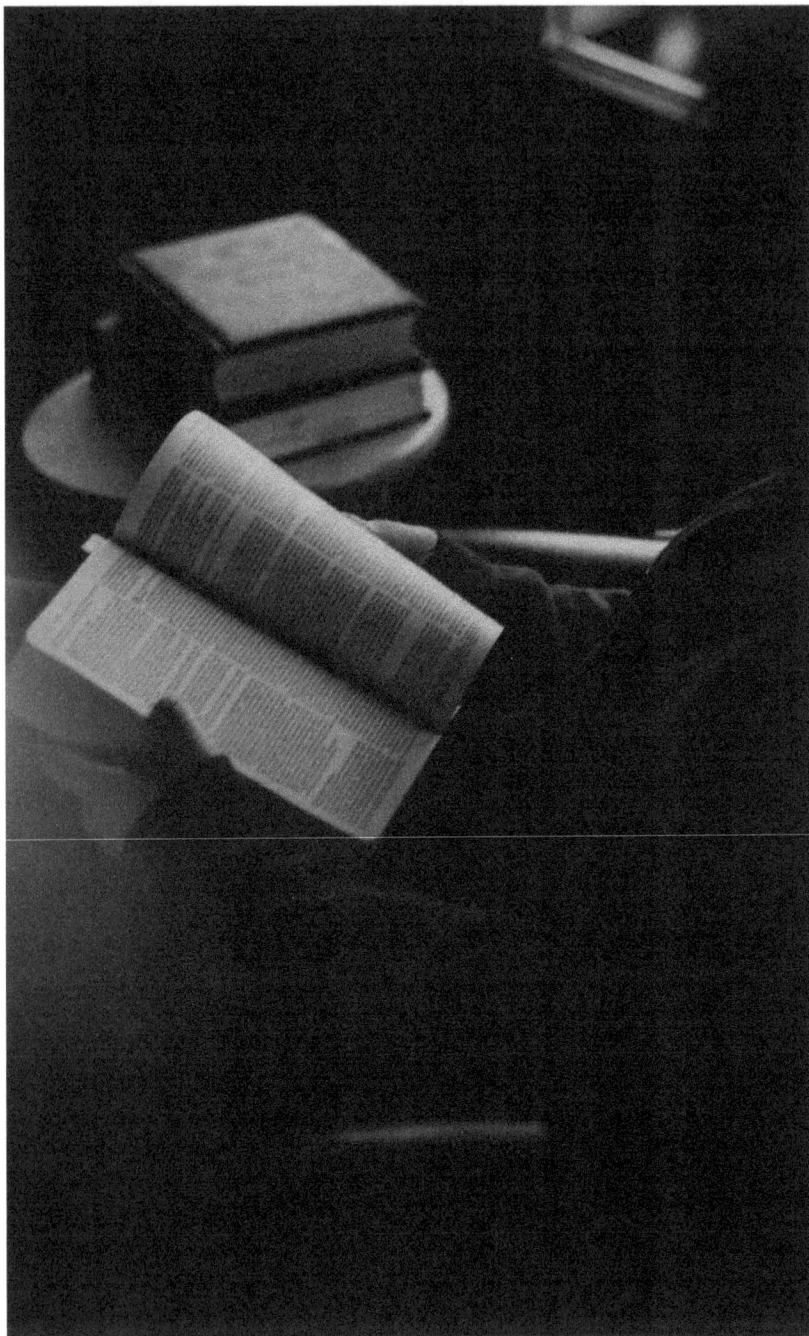

INTRODUCTION

Man has traveled to the moon and is sending rockets as far as possible of the Solar System and past. But then, regardless of all our advanced innovation and all our astonishing achievements, man despite everything remains a casualty to stress and anxiety – we keep on staying helpless to the requests of our fast-paced lives, which remove such a significant amount from us. The most exceedingly terrible of it is, a significant number of us don't understand how stressed out we are!

Anxiety and sadness have become a typical unwanted twin; today, it is nothing astonishing to discover somebody who is experiencing mental treatment for these issues. There is nothing amiss with it, clearly – actually, these individuals are to be commended on the grounds that they comprehended that they were in a difficult situation and went to find support! Many of us will not agree that we need assistance, let alone attempt to search it out.

In all actuality, regardless of how diligently we attempt, it is difficult to escape from anxiety. Our lives are so quick paced, so requesting, and it becomes something as standard, and every day as brushing our teeth. Sadly, the more you let this go unchecked, the more the number of sick impacts it will have on your well-being. Presently, it's anything but a completely sad errand; as troublesome as it may be, you can assume responsibility for anxiety!

Anxiety need not be your most exceedingly awful adversary; it need not affect your well-being, and it need not be articulated to such an extent that it winds up leaving you in a condition of clinical despondency. What you have to do is to assume responsibility for your own life and turn it around – Anxiety can be controlled and kept to a reasonable level! It isn't precisely the unconquerable obstruction it is by all accounts!

In this book, I have given you some snappy pointers on the most proficient method to deal with anxiety and deal with your fits of anxiety. You can wrestle the control of your life away from these tremendous sufferings that life appears to be throwing your way – simply follow the straightforward tips and lessons written inside these pages, and you will end up having the option to overcome and even beat anxiety!

Many thanks to you for picking this book! I trust it will be useful for you!

CHAPTER ONE:
HOW TO TREAT ANXIETY NATURALLY

Numerous individuals have interminable pressure and anxiety. They face side effects, for example, anxiety, fomentation, strain, a hustling heart, and chest torment. Indeed, anxiety is among the most well-known emotional well-being issues. In the United States, in excess of 18 percent of grown-ups are influenced by anxiety issues every year. At times, another wellbeing condition, for example, an overactive thyroid, can prompt an anxiety issue. Getting a precise determination can guarantee that an individual gets the best treatment.

In this chapter, you will find out about a wide scope of regular and home cures that can help with pressure and anxiety.

Regular solutions for anxiety and stress

Common cures are commonly protected to use close by progressively customary clinical treatments. Be that as it may, adjustments to the eating routine and some common supplements can change the way antianxiety medications work, so it is fundamental to counsel a specialist before attempting these arrangements. The specialist may likewise have the option to suggest other regular cures.

1. Exercise

Exercise may assist in treating anxiety. Exercise is an extraordinary method to consume off anxious vitality, and research will, in general, help this utilization. For instance, a 2015 audit of 12 randomized controlled preliminaries found that exercise might be a treatment for anxiety. Nonetheless, the survey advised that lone research of higher caliber could decide how successful it is. Exercise may likewise help with anxiety brought about by upsetting conditions. Consequences of a recent report, for instance, propose that exercise can profit individuals with anxiety identified with stopping smoking.

2. Reflection

Reflection can assist with easing back dashing contemplations, making it simpler to oversee pressure and anxiety. A wide scope of reflection styles, including care and contemplation during yoga, may help. Mindfulness-based cognitive therapy is progressively mainstream in treatment. A 2010 meta-expository survey proposes that it tends to be exceptionally viable for individuals with clutters identifying with state of mind and anxiety.

3. Relaxation exercises

A few people unwittingly tense the muscles and grip the jaw in light of anxiety. Dynamic relaxation exercises can help. Have a go at lying in an agreeable position and gradually tightening and loosening up each muscle gathering, starting with the toes and working up to the shoulders and jaw.

4. Writing

Figuring out how to communicate anxiety can cause it to feel progressively sensible. Some exploration recommends that journaling and different types of composing can help individuals to adapt better to anxiety. A recent report, for instance, found that experimental writing may support kids and youngsters to oversee anxiety.

5. Time management strategies

A few people feel anxious if they have such a large number of duties without a moment's delay. These may include family, work, and wellbeing related exercises. Having an arrangement set up for the following important activity can assist with keeping this anxiety under control. Successful time management strategies can help individuals to concentrate on each undertaking in turn. Book-based organizers and online schedules can help, as can fighting the temptation to perform multiple tasks. A few people find that separating significant undertakings into sensible advances can assist them with accomplishing those assignments with less pressure.

6. Aromatherapy

Smelling calming plant oils can assist with facilitating pressure and anxiety. Certain aromas work preferable for certain individuals over others, so consider trying different things with different choices. Lavender might be particularly useful. A recent report tried the impacts of aromatherapy with lavender on a sleeping disorder in 67 ladies matured 45–55. Results propose that the aromatherapy may lessen the pulse for the time being and help to ease rest issues in the long haul.

7. Cannabidiol oil

CBD oil originates from the cannabis plant. Cannabidiol (CBD) oil is a subsidiary of the cannabis, or weed, plant. In contrast to different types of marijuana, CBD oil doesn't contain tetrahydrocannabinol, or THC, which is the substance that makes a "high." CBD oil is promptly accessible without a solution in numerous elective human services shops. Fundamental research proposes that it can possibly lessen anxiety and frenzy. In zones where clinical weed is lawful, specialists may likewise have the option to endorse the oil.

8. Herbal teas

Numerous herbal teas guarantee to help without breaking a sweat rest. A few people discover the way toward making and drinking tea mitigating, yet a few teas may have a more straightforward impact on the mind that outcomes in diminished anxiety. Consequences of a little 2018 preliminary propose that chamomile can modify levels of cortisol, a pressure hormone.

9. Herbal supplements

Like herbal teas, numerous herbal supplements guarantee to lessen anxiety. In any case, minimal logical proof backings these cases. It is crucial to work with a specialist who is proficient in herbal supplements and their potential connections with different medications.

10. Time with pets

Pets offer friendship, love, and backing. Research distributed in 2018 affirmed that pets could be helpful to individuals with an assortment of psychological wellness issues, including anxiety. While numerous individuals lean toward felines, hounds, and other little warm-blooded animals, individuals with hypersensitivities will be satisfied to discover that the pet has to be fuzzy to offer help. A recent report found that thinking about crickets could improve mental wellbeing in more established individuals. Investing energy with creatures can likewise diminish anxiety and stress-related to injury. Aftereffects of a 2015 orderly survey propose that prepping and investing energy with ponies can reduce a portion of these impacts. The anxiety that is constant or meddles with an individual's capacity to work warrants treatment.

When there is no fundamental ailment, for example, a thyroid issue, treatment is the most well-known type of treatment. Treatment can assist an individual in understanding what triggers their anxiety. It can likewise help with making a positive way of life changes and working through an injury.

One of the best treatments for anxiety is called Cognitive Behavioural Therapy (CBT). The objective is to enable an individual to see how their contemplations influence their feelings and conduct and to supplant those responses with positive or productive other options. CBT can help with summed up anxiety and anxiety identifying with a particular issue, for example, work or an occasion of injury.

Medication can likewise assist an individual with managing incessant anxiety. A specialist may recommend medications in any of the accompanying gatherings:

- Antianxiety drugs called benzodiazepines, including Xanax and valium
- Antidepressants called particular serotonin reuptake inhibitors, including Prozac
- Sleeping medications, if anxiety meddles with rest

Normal anxiety cures can supplant or supplement conventional medications.

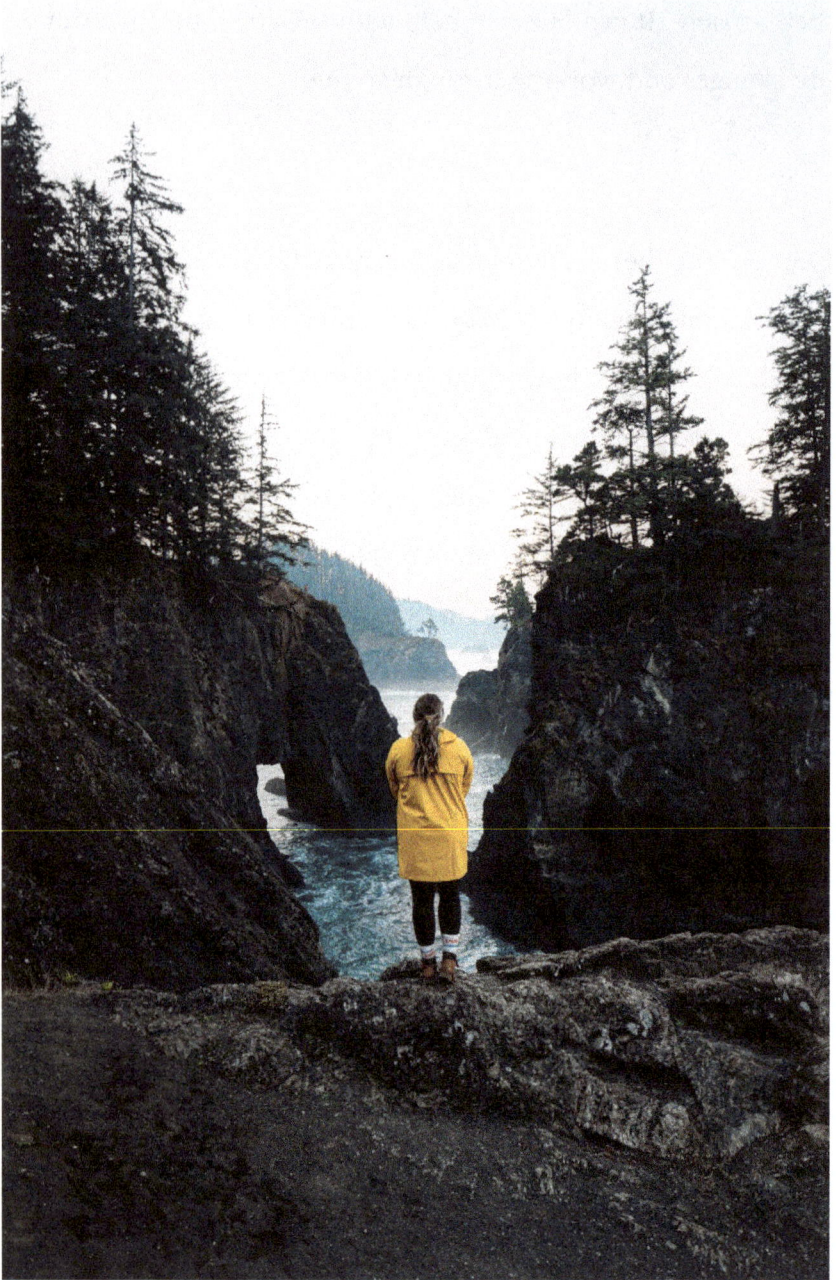

CHAPTER TWO: EFFECTIVE TIPS ON HOW TO DEAL WITH ANXIETY AND PROCRASTINATION

In this chapter, we will look at how to avoid procrastination and ensuring that you do not develop that late minute rush and anxiety over your tasks. Sometimes, we feel there is a lot of time on our hands to do our jobs. However, we end up procrastinating and not doing our best the deliver on the said task. I will be explaining detailed steps on how to handle our time better, deal with distractions, and ultimately reduce stress and anxiety in our daily lives. Here goes:

Stage 1: Start the task.

Get moving, regardless of whether you have failed previously. If you plan to win, you should start. This appears glaringly evident; however, if you have been procrastinating on something, that is the best time to start it. This step will show that it has taken the first grand step to become very successful in life

Stage 2: Set out a deadline to get the job done

We will talk about this point in more detail in a later area in this part. The odds are remote that you will ever complete anything without it getting booked into your schedule. We always wait because we don't close off the first time to complete the activity.

Stage 3: Break the activity into small parts

You will never begin shedding pounds if you see the entire project in one gym session. A heavy drinker would experience issues envisioning himself not drinking for the remainder of his/her life. Anybody can deal with not drinking for 24 hours. "one day, one step at a time" is a famous slogan among self-help groups. It is the acknowledgment of a critical truth of our experience: We live our whole lives in the here and now. What else will we do with it?.

Stage 4. Embrace a 'Do it now' mindset.

Individuals who overcome procrastination issues figure out how to progress toward becoming 'Do It Now'ers.' They never hold up until tomorrow to do what they know ought to be done today. They set things back after each use. They won't delay.

Stage 5. Set destinations.

We all know the important requirements for setting goals for our everyday life, but we must repeat it here because it affects our ability to stop procrastinating. Set a goal to accomplish something you have procrastinated about doing today.

Stage 6. Audit your achievements.

Successful people in life harp on their small wins. Losers always center around their disappointments. It is of incentive to help yourself to remember zones where you have prevailing with regards to winning the hesitation game.

Stage 7. Reward or rebuff yourself.

I am not supporting immoral conduct by proposing you overcome procrastinating issues by rebuffing yourself. What I am recommending is that you discover an effective method for punishing yourself for the practices that aid procrastination in your life. For example, not accomplishing things you said you would do in record time. One supervisor I know purchases his staff lunch out of his pocket if he doesn't have his reports on a schedule. If he vows to convey something and hesitates, at that point, he needs to fork out money, and for him, this is negative support for negative conduct.

Also, if you have prevailed with regards to carrying out a responsibility you have since quite a while ago procrastinated about doing, compensate yourself. We will, in general, recurrent those practices for which we get encouraging feedback and disregard those practices, which result in negative fortification.

TAKING CARE OF DISTRACTIONS

If interruptions become an issue for you, utilize the five stages recorded below. To figure out what is an issue with disruption, ask yourself, "Am I accepting small interruptions during high-priority moments of my life?" In this way, practice these means to check the time wasted while attending to such interruptions.

Schedule the free days on your calendar

A lot of individuals think the only time you are genuinely 'occupied' is the point at which you have somebody with you. A secretary checked her Supervisor's office, sees nobody, and erroneously assumes he/she is less busy. There is nothing wrong with scheduling time in your everyday organizer that will enable you to maintain a strategic distance from the time-squandering movement called interferences.

Inform the people around you that you can't be interrupted

If you need to take out interruptions, ensure you have a 'no interference' periods in your daily schedule. Tell others you can't be disturbed in any way, shape, or form unless the office building is on fire! And only if the fire is moving toward the floor underneath you! Achieving your goals requires desperate measures, and this is just one of them.

Whenever you are interrupted, stand up.

Do you need a strategy guaranteed to reduce interruption time to the barest minimal? Stand up when an interrupter comes into the room and stay standing while they talk. They will before long get the message, 'Be quick I'm occupied.'

Let us analyze this example, "If somebody comes into your space to interrupt you and you welcome them in, and you sit in a relaxed position, put your feet up on the work area, and offer them a cup of coffee." What message would you say you are passing on to them? Of course, the message would look like this - "enter, take a seat, make yourself comfortable, and let's talk. What I was doing isn't so important; waste my time in any capacity you deem fit!"

Make fewer trips through the office.

This may appear to be somewhat simple, yet would you say you are mindful what amount of time is squandered in a day by running for an espresso, water, and the washroom? Become mindful that when you leave your work region. Your goals are more important than some side attractions.

60 PRACTICALTIMEMANAGEMENT TIPS TO HELP YOU REDUCE ANXIETY

1. When wiping out wardrobes, storerooms, and so forth., mark three containers: "scrap, give away, and keep."
2. If you haven't utilized something in over a year, don't give it a chance to occupy the prime room.

3. Schedule a 'tranquil hour' every day and think of it as non-debatable.

4. Try not to give others a chance to infringe on your significant "personal-time."

5. Each night, set out all that you will require in the first part of the day.

6. Utilize your arranging schedule to plan your schedules.

7. Calendar "arrangements" with yourself.

8. Have an office in your home for composing and recording.

9. Exploit self-inking stamps to spare time.

10. Agent at whatever point conceivable.

11. Complete things during the specified time.

12. Make meals in two-folds and freeze them to save you some cooking time.

13. Toss out however much correspondence and other administrative work as could reasonably be expected.

14. Store adornments in egg containers inside a cabinet.

15. Keep an inventory of every item used regularly, for example, paper products, lights, trash packs, paper cuts, Post-it Notes.

16. Settle on minor choices rapidly.

17. Try not to sit around anguishing after choices.

18. Store things near where they will be utilized. Duplicate if necessary.

19. Clean the bath during a shower. It is simpler working from within.

20. Keep work desk supplies in your briefcase, handbag, or vehicle for those eccentric deferrals and waiting periods.

21. Say 'no' more frequently and quit volunteering for everything.

22. Try not to continue rearranging paper. Handle each piece as it shows up.

23. Start your day before it dawns. Wake up early and plan your movements beginning of the day.

24. Try not to read passively. Search for new ideas. Use highlighters. Make short notes.

25. Try not to store magazines. Detach or photocopy the important part of the articles you will need.

26. Set a deadline for each project and endeavor to stick to it.

27. Always carry about a small jotter with you for note-taking.

28. Plan ahead of time your TV review time. It very well may be a continuous burglar.

29. Utilize hued names to signal significant dates in your arranging schedule and to feature earnest demands that surface.

30. Carry an inventory of Post-it Notes on your calendar.

31. Review your "junk mail" during your free time (for example, the last fifteen minutes of the day).

32. Take just lightweight suitcases while traveling via air. Delays can happen when hanging tight for your luggage to be cleared.

33. Utilize mostly transparent compartments for remains so you can see what you have in the fridge.

34. When leaving a message for somebody to get back to you, let them know the best time they can contact you.

35. If the individual you call isn't accessible, attempt to get the data you need from another person as opposed to leave a message.

36. Keep paper and pen helpful in each room.

37. Carry a versatile "Trident" 3-hole puncher in your folder case or meeting binder.

38. Record in your schedule the time by which you should go out (or hotel) If you have to attend any meeting at a far distance to get there in good time.

39. Have a lot of keys on you than you may think you will be needing.

40. Try not to be hooked on your phone. Utilize your answering machine to replying mail or voice messages, most especially to take messages during the supper hour or overlook the phone.

41. When masterminding doctor and dental specialist appointments, take the first slot of the morning so you can

be quickly attended to and stay ahead of the crows at the hospital.

42. Keep a stock of welcome cards, stamps, and gifts close by.

43. Set away materials after use. Tidy up the mess as it's created.

44. Utilize a highlighter when reading letters and reports so you can check those parts requiring action.

45. Continuously check in with appointments; don't assume the fellow at the other end will remember.

46. Use stacking plate to sort mail as to charges, correspondence, garbage mail.

47. Spot shading dabs on the entirety of your charge cards for simple distinguishing proof.

48. Photocopy the two sides of your Mastercards (around nine for every page) and leave a duplicate in your home sheltered and safe storage box.

49. Utilize the driving time to tune in to tape tapes or CDs.

50. Record thoughts from tape tapes or CDs by managing them into a pocket recorder.

51. Keep a pocket recorder in your vehicle for chronicle thoughts, data, activities, and so on., as they strike you.

52. Buy into bulletins identified with your calling to eliminate understanding time.

53. Shading your different keys with little plastic rings, accessible in numerous stores, to avoid mishandling.

54. Photocopy birth certificates, marriage declarations, and so forth., and keep them in your documents.

55. Structure the habit for taking your arranging schedule with you any place you go – even in the midst of a get-away. You can record that ports-of-call, most loved cafés, lodgings, and individuals you meet.

56. Store void garments holders on one side of the storeroom and use it as required. Try not to give them a chance to blend with the ones being utilized.

57. Keep your personal belongings tote sack outfitted with every single personal thing, from the toothbrush to travel hairdryer, and use it only when you are about to go on a trip.

58. Discover approaches to delegate functions to people around you.

59. Keep your phone calls as short as possible.

60. Place a call through instead of chatting away for long hours.

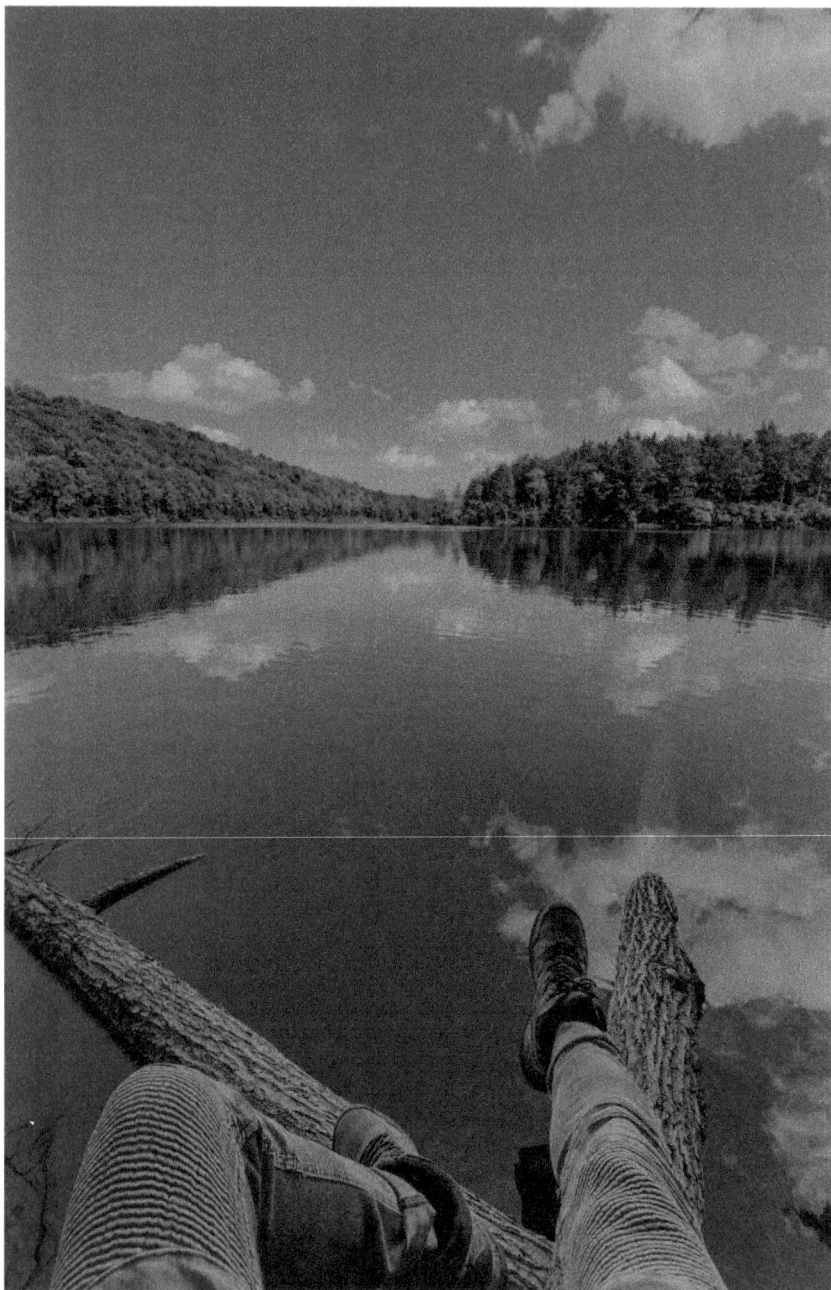

CHAPTER THREE: MANAGING VARIOUS BODY SENSATIONS DURING ANXIETY – CONTROLLED BREATHING

Breathing comes naturally-we can all do it, and we don't have to worry about it. But it's like standing or walking – if you don't watch your posture, you can end up with problems; if you pay attention to it, you can prevent all sorts of discomfort. Breathing changes when we get stressed out – it gets short and shallow, and we inhale a lot of oxygen. After you've just raced to catch a bus or race to get to an appointment on time, you will find yourself doing this – it's a perfectly natural reaction to exertion and also stress, and it's called hyperventilation.

When we're tense or exercising, we all hyperventilate. At these times, breathing faster gets oxygen to our muscles so that our body is ready for action – for example, running away. Rapid breathing is not a short-term problem – in fact, if you've just run to catch a bus, your body will need extra oxygen – but if you keep over-breathing, you'll be forcing too much oxygen into the bloodstream, and this will disrupt the delicate oxygen-carbon dioxide balance. Your body will tell you that things went out of sync by triggering unpleasant physical sensations such as:

- Face tingling, hands or extremities
- Cramps and muscle tremors
- Vision problems and dizziness
- Difficulty in breathing
- Exhaustion, and tiredness
- Stomach and chest pains

You won't get all these symptoms necessarily, but even one or two of these sensations can be very alarming. They often trigger more anxiety, and thus more hyperventilation: a vicious cycle. This stress cycle can sometimes-but not always-lead to a panic attack.

So far, this probably sounds quite dramatic – and if you're stuck in a panic cycle, then it'll feel dramatic – but the good news is that you can easily learn how to correct rapid breathing and control the symptoms by developing the regular breathing skills for yourself. This means learning to breathe gently and evenly through your nose, complete filling your lungs, and then exhaling slowly and completely. Below is a sketch of a breathing exercise that will help you take control of the hyperventilation symptoms, and you'll see that it's really quite simple. The key to using it is to be so practiced in the technique that, even when stressed, you can switch to it whenever you need to.

Regularly breathing: How to do it

Before you start, first, a few guidelines:

- Use your lungs completely, and avoid breathing alone from your upper chest

- Respire smoothly, without gulping or throbbing

- Do this exercise lying down when you first practice so you may feel better the difference between shallow and deep breathing. You can try the exercise sitting and standing later as you become more practiced. Eventually, you can do that even while you're walking

- Place one hand on the chest and the other on the stomach

- Have your stomach swell as you breathe in through your nose. This ensures you are making good use of your lungs. Try to minimize the movement in your upper chest and maintain gentle movement

- Breathe out slowly and evenly through your nose

- Repeat that and try to get a rhythm going. You 're aiming to take eight to twelve breaths per minute: it counts as one breath to breathe in and out. At first, this may be difficult to measure, so practice for a complete breathing cycle counting five to seven seconds (i.e., one inhalation and one exhalation)

- Do not take a quick, deep breath

- Controlled breathing in action: Panic attack management

Difficulties With Controlled Respiration

When trying out some of the coping strategies in this book, it's normal to have a few 'glitches.' That's probably going to be the case when you try to regulate your breathing, so I've mentioned a few common problems and their solutions below.

Difficulties in breathing naturally and comfortably

The smooth, regular breathing may not come naturally at first, and you might feel it is awkward and uncomfortable. You may feel you don't get enough air or that the air doesn't actually fill your lungs. This is all fairly common. However, with practice, you'll find that this slower breathing rate becomes easier and is actually quite comfortable. Often you just have to give yourself time to develop the skill. If you keep on feeling you can't fully breathe in, start the exercise by exhaling as much as possible. You should empty your lungs in this way, and the first in-breath will be deep and soothing.

Feeling weird during practice

You are probably very prone to physical stimuli, and now you are trying something different that affects the physical way you feel. You are bound to be very conscious of even slight physical changes, and some new sensations associated with controlled breathing will occur. These are not going to be harmful; they are going to be just new for you. Try to be curious about them-just watch them see what's going on if you consider them to start the work.

Forget about practicing

This may be the most common problem, but I can't stress enough how important it is to practice the exercise whenever you can – you 're trying to develop a new habit that will come only through repeated rehearsals. Try using reminders to help you practice: a regular alarm on your mobile phone, a colored mark on your calendar, whatever you know from time to time will catch your attention. Most of us take a regular look at our watches throughout the day, so you might find it helpful to put a little eye-catching mark on your watch (I used a small blob of nail varnish).

Be assured that as your skill improves, you'll find it easier and easier to switch to controlled breathing whenever you need to, and it will even become a habit of correcting your breathing as it starts getting too fast.

CHAPTER FOUR: MANAGING VARIOUS BODY SENSATIONS DURING ANXIETY – APPLIED RELAXATION

The muscles in our bodies get tensed under stress: that is normal. However, if it is exaggerated or if it goes on too long, an enormous amount of unpleasant feelings may be caused by muscle stress. You'll notice that all of our bodies have muscles, and we can encounter tension-related aches and pains almost everywhere in our bodies. Not everyone feels these feelings, but they typically include:

• Stiff collar

• Wretched hands

• Chest high.

• Trouble breathing

• Shivering

• Stomach upset

• Trouble swallowing

• Blurred vision

• Pain in the back

Naturally, when these sensations become distressing, they can trigger more tension and so the vicious cycle is set up for our old enemy. Learning how to relax in response to it is the most effective way of controlling body tension: to 'apply' relaxation as and when we need it. Simple to say but still difficult to do. This 'applied' relaxation is not just about sitting in front of the TV or getting a hobby (although these recreations are valuable too); learning applied relaxation means acquiring a skill that helps you to relieve physical stress anytime you need it. With time, you will become confident in reducing your anxiety and tensions in a variety of situations – in effect, when you need it, you will have a portable skill to use. Even better, you'll find that your mind will always begin to relax when your body is pain-free. And it's worth taking the time to learn how to relax in all.

However, it takes time-the ability to relax at will is achieved only through practice, practice, and a little more practice. One of the most effective ways to master the skill is through a series of structured exercises, such as the four below, working your way. These are designed to help you slowly learn how to relax. The first two routines are pretty long, and you may find that the instructions recorded are helpful. Following the relaxation instructions, you should do your own recording (see pages 370–80). Be sure to use soft, gentle speech to give yourself the best chance to relax – if you bark successful orders on yourself, you won't find it very relaxing!

Guidelines for Relaxation

You 're not going to be able to relax and read the instructions at the same time, so get acquainted with all the exercises first – you 're going to see that they're getting shorter and shorter, so that might spur you on! Once you know the routines, you can start working through them one at a time. When the first exercise allows you to relax, move on to exercise two; when you've mastered this, start exercise three. By the time you exercise four, you'll be ready to learn a very brief, quick relaxation routine that will fit easily into your daily lives. This entire learning cycle of a series of exercises should be performed slowly, perhaps over a few weeks. Of course, the length of time needed will vary from person to person, so don't worry that you're not making rapid enough progress – this will only make you more tense – and don't try to rush things. Only move on to the next exercise at the end of a routine when you feel completely relaxed.

Some 'top tips' before you get started:

- Plan your exercise. Try to get a routine going every day and keep to the same time. In this way, you will have a better chance of continuing the practice

- Practise often. Practice at least twice a day: the better you exercise, the better it is to relax at will, and that is your objective.

- Choose the right place: practice in a quiet place where there is no disturbance to you. Make sure it doesn't get too hot or too chilly. Offer yourself the best chance to unwind

- Pick the right time: do not relax when you feel very tired, or when you are either hungry or full. Under those circumstances, it is difficult to relax

- Get relaxed: when you want to relax first, make sure you find a comfortable spot and wear comfortable clothes. You probably start by lying down, but you can practice sitting or even standing water.

- Get into the right mindset: try to be 'passive.' This doesn't mean you're concerned about your results but just having a look. Be curious to see how things are going; don't judge yourself

- Just breathe! During your relaxation practice, it's so important not to hold your breath or hyperventilate; if you do, you might feel worse rather than better. Remember to breathe through your nose, completely filling your lungs, so you feel your stomach stretching a bit. Keep the tempo slow and steady. Before you start your relaxation training, it is best to get the hang of regulated breathing (see Chapter 8) and then you can be confident that you are breathing in a manner that will help, not hinder

- Record progress. To keep track of your progress, use a sheet such as a Diary. You can expect a certain amount of daily variation (as we all have ups and downs in our tension levels), but you'll be able to see patterns by keeping a log over time, and then you'll be able to work out what makes relaxation easier or harder. The more you understand about your physical tensions, the more you will have control over them

- Stay tuned! I emphasized this so much that this final 'top tip' you probably predicted. But the fact that practice will boost your skills doesn't get round

Relaxation workouts

Now, the exercises. There are four main exercises;

- Lengthy relaxation

- Shortened relaxation

- Simple relaxation

- Applied relaxation

You will see that the first exercise requires a great deal of time, and effort but the investment is worth it. The skills you are learning are the basis for the brief, applied relaxation that will enable you to counteract tension as and when you need to.

Lengthy relaxation (LR)

This lengthy relaxation is based on a very well-established relaxation routine developed in the 1930s by Edmund Jacobsen – so you can feel confident this is a tried and tested routinely. His aim was to develop a systematic program to help his patients attain a deep relaxation level. His solution was a series of 'tense-then-relax' exercises that focused on the main muscle groups in the body. Another advantage of this approach is that it helps us learn how to distinguish between tense muscles and relaxed ones. We can sometimes get so used to being tense that we don't even realize we are. These exercises help us recognize when we're tense – and when we do that, in response, we can relax.

The basic motion you use at each stage of the exercise is as follows:

• Stress the muscles but don't strain: emphasis on feeling pain.

• Hold this for about 5 seconds, then let the tension off for 10-15 seconds

• Focus on how your muscles feel when relaxing: notice the difference between tense muscles and relaxed muscles

LR asks you to do this throughout the body for many different sets of muscle groups, so it's really a very thorough exercise. Breathing between each stage in the procedure and during the exercise is important, slowly and regularly. When you've decided where and when you'll be doing your exercises, get comfortable, and start focusing on your body parts as follows:

- **The Feet**: Squeeze your toes back, tense your feet muscles. Relax and then repeat.
- **Legs**: Straighten the legs, point the toes towards the face. Relax and let the legs go limp and repeat.

- **Abdomen:** Tense your stomach muscles by pulling them in and up – as if you were preparing to get a punch. Relax and then repeat.

- **Back:** Arch your back. Relax and then repeat.

- **Shoulders/neck**: Shrug your shoulders, up and in. Press the back of your head. Relax and then repeat.

- **Arms**: Stretch hands and arms out. Relax and unwind. Let the arms hang limp. Repeat.

- Face: Tense the forehead and the jaw. Lower and bite your eyebrows. Relax and then repeat.

- The entire body Tense: your whole body: feet, legs, abdomen, back, neck and shoulders, arms, and face. Keep stress for a couple of seconds. Relax and then repeat.

At the end of the routine, some of us still feel tense-if this is for you, just go through it again. Just repeat the exercise in those areas if only parts of your body feel tense. If it is very painful or distressing to tense and concentrates on other muscle groups, then skip that group for now and prepare to go back to it later when you have more faith and relaxation skills. The important thing about your performance isn't stress.

When the exercise is over, and you feel relaxed, spend a few moments relaxing your mind. Think of a restful thing: Whatever scene or image works best for you. Breathe through your nose slowly, filling up your lungs as thoroughly as you can. Go on for one or two minutes, then open your eyes. Don't stand up straight away; just move slowly when you're ready and stretch gently. Feel good. Feel good.

Long relaxation should be practiced about twice a day until at the end of the exercise, you always feel completely relaxed. You can then move on to the shortened LR, which is adapted. Remember learning how to relax takes time. Offer yourself a chance, and don't expect it to succeed too soon. As we said earlier if they have written instructions to direct them, some people find it easier to follow this exercise. Know, reading the relaxation script at the end of the book will make your own audio recording. Make sure you speak slowly and gently; you aim to be calm.

Shortened relaxation

Once you've mastered LR, you can start shortening the relaxation routine simply by losing out on the 'tense' level. Simply go through the familiar sequence, but just relax the various muscle groups one at a time (no tensing). You can switch to the next level, which is modifying the routine to be used at other times and in other locations if you can do this effectively. You may try the exercise sitting, for example, rather than lying down, or you may move from a quiet bedroom to a less peaceful living area. In this way, you'll learn to relax in a variety of different places, and that's what you need to cope with in real-life.

Simple relaxation

This is an exercise that you can practice even shorter as you become more experienced in achieving a relaxed state. It is based on the exercise a cardiologist named Herbert Benson had developed in the 1970s. He just wanted to help his heart patients reduce their stress levels, but the exercise has established itself as a technique of relaxation that is universally useful. You'll need to find a restful 'mental device' for the exercise to use during the routine. This means finding a soothing sound or phrase, or image. You might use the word 'calm' or the sound of the sea, or the image of a relaxing object, maybe a picture or an ornament you like, or a scene you find calming, like a quiet country spot or a deserted beach. It doesn't have to be complicated: it's best sometimes to get easy.

Follow those guidelines when you've figured out what's most important for you:

- Seat comfortably with your eyes closed. Imagine getting heavier and more relaxed on your body.

- Breathe through the nose and be aware of your breathing while you inhale. Think about your mental image as you breathe out whilst breathing easily and naturally.

- Don't worry if you're good at the workout or not; just let go of your tensions and relax at your own pace. Distracting thoughts are likely to get into your mind. Do not worry about this and dwell on them; just go back to thinking about your mental image or breathing pattern.

- You can keep that going for as long as you need to feel relaxed. This could be two or twenty minutes: the criterion for completing the exercise is that you feel relaxed. When you stop, sit still for a few moments with your eyes closed and then sit with your eyes open. Don't stand up or start moving too fast.

Since this is a brief exercise, you can do it more often than the previous ones. You could do it every hour for a minute or two; or at breaks in coffee, lunch, and tea, or between appointments, or at any service station if you are driving on a long journey and feel stressed. The options are endless and discovering a regular routine that fits your lifestyle is the most useful thing you can do.

Cued relaxation

By now, you 're going to be familiar with three relaxation techniques, so if you've been practicing, you 're going to learn more and more relaxation skills. Once you have mastered the first three exercises, you can start using your relaxation skills throughout the day, and not just at the 'relaxation time' you have designated. You will thus become better and better at being able to relax at will. You'll need to start by learning how to relax 'on cue,' and everything you need to relax is something that catches your eyes regularly and reminds you to:

• Put your shoulders down

• Relax your body muscles

• Test your breathing

• Sit back and relax

You may use something you look at frequently during the day as a prompt, or as a reminder – your watch, an office clock, your Diary, for example. You'll be reminded to relax each time you see the cue, and so you'll practice your relaxation skills several times a day. There are all kinds of hints you could use; just work out what often catches your eye and use this as a reminder.

Applied Relaxation – The grand stage

The final stage of relaxation training is learning to practice it whenever you need it, using stress as your basis for action. You have to start trying it out during your day-to-day activities to do this. Start with situations that aren't too stressful, if possible, then work to more challenging situations as your skill and confidence improve. Relaxation will become a way of life with time and daily practice, and you'll find that you can relax just when you need to. Of course, you're bound to keep experiencing some tension from time to time – that's normal – but now you're going to have a better awareness of it, and you're going to have the skills to bring it under control.

You've been given the message throughout this chapter that relaxation is a skill, and therefore, it takes time to develop it – don't skimp on the effort you put in learning how to do it properly. Learning to play the piano is a useful analogy for relaxation training. Starting with the laborious but necessary scales (long relaxation), you would graduate to arpeggios (shortened relaxation). With this as a foundation, you could play simple tunes (simple relaxation) and gradually more sophisticated music (relaxation with cooking). You will only be able to sit at a piano after a lot of practice and play naturally (applied relaxation). If you had not worked through the earlier stages, you wouldn't be able to play spontaneously; and you might find that you can't relax when you need to if you haven't done the groundwork.

Difficulties in relaxation

If you find that as you work through your relaxation training, you have any problems, then you are not alone. Below are a few common hindrances:

Peculiar sensations when doing the exercises

It's usual to feel weird when you're doing something physical you're not used to doing. Don't worry about that (as if you do, your tension will only increase). The first time my tutor took us through a relaxation exercise, I remember feeling tense and annoyed, but now I find being able to relax is effective and invaluable. Seek to understand that a few practice sessions must take place before you start to feel confident with the exercises, and you will soon find that the odd or distracting sensations will vanish. Also, make sure that during the exercise, you are not hyperventilating (over-breathing), or standing up and moving too soon, or practicing when you are too hungry or full, as any of these things can cause unpleasant feelings.

Cramping

It can be painful, but it can never be dangerous. There are a couple of things that you can try to make it less likely to get cramped: avoid tensing your muscles too vigorously, especially avoid pointing your toes too enthusiastically. Try not to exercise when your muscles are cold, and use your practice in a warm room. If you get a cramp, relieve the discomfort by soothing the affected muscle gently and take a break from the workout – you can still come back to it later.

Fall asleep

Sometimes this isn't a problem – that's what you're hoping for – but if you don't want to fall asleep, you can try sitting down instead of lying down, you can time your exercise so you won't get tired when you start, you could hold something (unbreakable), so you'd drop it down and wake up if you dozed off.

Intruding and anxious thoughts

The human brain has evolved to give us the ability to think creatively and have many ideas. That's great, but it means we 're all getting lots of thoughts intruding on our consciousness. So when other things disrupt your relaxation, don't worry, as this is very natural and not a significant obstacle to your practice. The best way to make sure undesirable thoughts go away is by not dwelling on them. Accept that from time to time, they drift into your mind and then simply focus on your relaxation exercise. If you're not trying to think about them, they won't go away. If I tell you not to think about a pink car, you're likely to get an image of a pink car in your mind immediately; and if I stress: 'No really, clear your mind about pink cars,' then the image will probably become even more fixed. Only tell yourself that having intrusions is natural. Do not pay much attention to them, and simply turn your thoughts back to relaxation.

Does not feel comfortable

This can be an issue when you start the relaxation training first. You may not get any benefit when you're new to the workout because the benefits come with the practice. The most important thing is not to try too hard as tension will result. Let the relaxing sensations just happen when they happen. It's also worth asking yourself if you are in the right state of mind (or body) to relax and if your surroundings are appropriate. If not, later or somewhere else, do the exercise-give yourself the best chance to succeed.

Note This!

Taking exercise is a very effective way to unwind physically. For whatever reason, if you can't get on with the relaxation exercises, you could try to do something physically demanding, as this will always reduce muscle tension. It's also a good way to distract us from the worries, especially if we have to focus on rules or techniques (for example, playing squash or taking a dance class). Another wonderful thing about exercise is feeling a sense of superiority as well as improved self-confidence.

If you are worried about the physical symptoms of anxiety, exercising means you can bring in controlled feelings of breathlessness, a racing heart, and other physical sensations, and you can be confident that these responses will come and go without harming you. It puts you inside.

Research in recent years has shown us the particular benefits of exercise for managing stress and anxiety. Most importantly, regular exercise seems to raise the 'fight-flight threshold,' which means it takes more to get us stressed, which in turn means we're more comfortable with it. Physical activity also seems to be fighting the effects of stress on the brain itself (by bathing it in a cocktail of 'good' neurochemicals) and lowering blood pressure: this is very reassuring if you are worried that long-term stress may affect your health. The 'cocktail of good neurochemicals' also improves our mood, and this again helps in stress management because the more hopeful and capable we are, the better our moods. And the benefits of exercise don't end there, as regular exercise accelerates our learning ability, and an improved memory usually means we 're that bit more confident and a bit less anxious. So what these findings also suggest is that if you did regular exercise while working your way through it, you would get more out of this program.

In short, much research now supports the correlation between exercise and reduced anxiety and stress, so it's really worth thinking about becoming more involved. And it's always worth talking about enjoying yourself while you're doing this: cycling or running in a lovely place, going to the gym with your best friend, taking a fun fitness class-doing anything you want to work into your life.

Yoga

Yoga combines the use of meditation, breathing exercises, physical posturing, and a distinct philosophy. Studies have shown that performing yoga and other physical types of exercise can help lower heart rate, blood pressure, and can also help reduce depression and anxiety symptoms. Daily yoga will help you stay calm and comfortable as you go about your everyday life. It can also help you find the strength to face events as they happen without feeling anxious or restless. The use of asanas, which are body postures, pranayama's, which are breathing exercises, meditation, and the philosophy of ancient yoga, involved the practice of yoga to the greatest benefit. It has been shown to help people with social anxiety disorder carry on their lives in a more confident and happier manner, with a more optimistic outlook on life.

The techniques that follow can help you calm your mind and say hello to a new and positive you. The best way to do that is to go to a yoga class and properly learn the techniques.

• Use asanas to shift your body and extricate your mind from tension. Learn how to eliminate stress and negativity from your whole body by performing these yoga poses:

- Dhanurasana-The Bow

- Matyasana-Pose of the Fish

- Janu Shirsasana – Forward One-Legged Bend

- Setubandhasana-Pose Bridge

- Marjariasana-a stretch of cat

- Paschimottanasana – The Steady Bend

- Hastapadasana – The Steady Bend

- Adhomukha Shwanasana-the dog looking down

- Shirshasana-Headquarters

- Shavasana – Pose of the Corpse

Lie down in the Nidra Yoga when you've completed the asanas session or yoga poses, and give your body and mind a chance to relax. This is useful in flushing out body toxins, one of the greatest causes of stress.

• Use pranayama's to relive fear and relax properly. You can free the clutter from your mind by focusing on your breath, get rid of the negative thoughts that cause anxiety, Learn the following pranayamas:

- Kapal Bhati Pranayama – Skull Sparkling Technique of Breathing

- Pranayama Bhastrika

- Nadi Shodha Pranayama – Alternative Nostril Breathing – This is highly effective in relieving tension, as exhalation is longer than inhalation

- Bhramari Pranayama-Breath of the bee

Follow that with meditation to set the mind free. This is an excellent way to relax your mind, free it from distractions and give you a sense of peace and tranquillity. Observe how your mind functions daily, how it keeps you engaged in focusing on small and small things, and stop concentrating on the things that cause you anxiety. It may also help you to stop brooding about the future, to think about what might happen.

I have no doubt you heard the word 'adrenaline rush' This is what happens to us when anxiety sets in when you worry about a specific threat. Let's say you're about to walk into an adventure park on a thrilling trip. At the tie, your body's adrenaline hormone peaks, and that leads to a quick heartbeat, tensioning of your muscles, and profuse sweating. Scientific studies have shown that you can reduce how much of that hormone is actually produced if you participate in regular meditation.

Next, you need to study and apply the ancient principles of yoga in your everyday life. The principles are clear but profound, and they are the key to a long, prosperous, and safe life. The principle of Santosha can teach you the strong value of being fulfilled while the principle of Aprigrah will help you set aside feelings of envy, the need to have more things, all of which contribute to anxiety and stress. The Shaucha theory talks about the cleanliness of mind and body, and this is useful if the Thought of the infectious disease is one of the causes of your anxiety.

Finally, we get to pray. This is the best form of support and the reassurance you need to stay free from stress and anxiety. Developing a daily habit of Prayer will fill you with positivity, energy, and help your mind to calm down and still be Prayer instantly instills a sense of trust, positivity, and calmness. Think about how you can help others, instead of being rooted in the state of mind of "me and mine." Helping others can help relieve stress and anxiety and make you feel a lot happier.

Banish negative people from your life and circumstances. Keep yourself surrounded by other positive people, and you will find that your mind is lighter, happier, and your entire approach to life will be different.

CHAPTER FIVE: MANAGING PSYCHOLOGICAL SYMPTOMS OF ANXIETY

Distraction

You will learn techniques in this chapter and in the next to keep the psychological dimensions of stress, fear, and anxiety under control. This means managing the alarming thoughts and images which run our minds through. As you already know, cycles of worrying thoughts (or pictures of the mind) and growing anxiety can develop and maintain high tensions. For instance, at a party, a woman who blushes easily and has trouble speaking fluently could easily get worried about her social appearance (she might even have a mental image of herself being flustered and embarrassed) and this anxiety would make it even more likely that she would blush and find it difficult to speak: a cycle of social anxiety could develop. If a man was having slight chest pain and thought: 'This might be a heart attack! 'His levels of stress would go up, and he'd get tense. Increased muscle tension would then exacerbate the pain, and his thoughts could become even more alarming: 'This is a heart attack! 'The anxiety will get worse and create a loop of increasing stress and troubling thoughts. Changing the thoughts could break the cycle; it is obvious.

What do psychological signs trigger?

Sometimes you'll find it easy to catch what's going on through your mind, but sometimes you might just be aware of feeling anxiety or fear. It will seem like it is coming out of the blue as if there is no trigger. The relation between thoughts and feelings is so powerful that an emotional response sometimes tends to occur spontaneously without any apparent thoughts or images. This is natural and always happens. Without realizing why, you could walk by a bonfire or smell old paint, and feel content or fear. If you've really reflected on it, you might realize it's because the smells remind you of happy childhood firework display experiences or helping your grandpa in the shed or upsetting memories of being burnt or being told off to play with paint. It functions for sensations of pleasure and unpleasure. Even if this automatic response is a stress reaction, it's often no bad thing: when a car gets around the corner too quickly, you jump out of the way without seeming to think about it; when a child looks like he's about to stumble into a fire, you grab him without thinking about it. In fact, there is a chain of reasoning behind such actions; but it becomes so well established that it is almost as if we are 'short-circuiting' the process of conscious thinking and thus saving precious time in dangerous situations.

This 'short-circuiting' can also cause concern about issues. Imagine a woman walking joyfully around a church full of flowers. She suddenly gets anxious and feels she has to get out of the church. It is only later that she learns that her emotions were caused because she smelled chrysanthemums, and this brought her back to her childhood when she was frightened by her piano teacher, who always had a vase on the piano with them. She 'short-circuited' the process of reasoning and endured powerful feelings of distress, which she did not understand at the time.

Whether or not you can actually put your finger on the mental component of these anxiety cycles, they do drive our distress, so it's good to have some strategies to tackle worrying thoughts and images. There are, basically, two ways to interrupt the loops of troubling thoughts:

• A distraction that shifts our attention away from the cycle

• Testing which helps us to identify and examine exaggerated concerns

Entertainment

You 're probably so used to multi-tasking that discovering that we can only focus entirely on one thing at a time would be a shock, but it's real and we can use it to our benefit, as it means that if we turn our attention to something constructive or fun, we can divert ourselves from stressful thoughts and images. By using specific distraction techniques, you can break the cycle of worrying thoughts and avoid increasing your anxiety.

There are three basic distraction techniques, and you can customize these to suit your needs with a bit of effort.

- Physical Exercise
- Refocus
- Exercising mentally

As we go through each of these techniques of distraction, you need to think about how you can make them work for you-try to link them to your preferences and interests. You must also bear in mind that the key to successful distraction is to find something that needs a lot of attention, is very specific, and has some interest in you. If a task of distraction is too superficial, too vague, or too boring, it does not tend to be effective.

Physical exercise

Physical activity can be the simplest of the three exercises, and it's particularly useful when you're so overwhelmed that you can't even think straight. Using physical distraction simply means keeping yourself active when stressed. If you are physically occupied, you are less likely to dwell on anxious thoughts. There are so many ways to do it:

• Exercise like cycling, jogging, playing tennis, taking the dog for a stroll, etc. These kinds of activities are especially beneficial because they help to use the adrenaline that can otherwise make you feel tense and, as we have seen before, exercise is a powerful way to manage stress

• Taking on small social tasks: for instance, if you feel self-conscious at a party, you can be offering people drinks to keep you and your mind occupied.

• Homework: clearing cabinets, mowing lawns, garage reorganization. The list is endless, and the advantage of keeping yourself active in this way is that you will probably feel good about doing something you still needed to do. The activities don't have to be on a wide scale – it will also work to clean a handbag or reorganize a messy personal organizer

- Fiddling: A technique that's very simple and underestimated. It does not take a great deal of mental strength and can be very discreet. For example, if you sit in a waiting room feeling edgy and tense, you might wind and unwind a paper clip, or fold a sweet wrapper into an interesting shape, pull it apart and put a ballpoint pen together. Nevertheless, each task can absorb your attention enough to break the cycle of anxiety and feeling stressed

You'll need different activities in different situations, so make sure you've got several up your sleeve. You could play squash in the evening to take your mind off the stress of the day; take a short walk up and down the corridor when you're very tense at the office; reorganize your desk when you can't leave the office but are alone; unwind and rewind paper clips to take your anxiety off the edge in meetings or waiting room if your physical task requires some degree of mental effort, so much the better, because the effect of distraction will be stronger.

Refocusing

This means being distracted by paying a great deal of attention to the things around you. If you were in a crowded street you could try to count the number of men and women with blond hair, or look for certain objects in a shop window; listen to the conversations of others in a café (discreetly!) or study somebody's dress details (again discreetly!) or note the details of a poster on the wall. The job doesn't have to be complex or sophisticated; to consume your attention, and you just need to find a variety of items. For example, if someone was nervous about using the supermarket, they might read car number plates while their friend took them to the store, attend their shopping list closely when going around the supermarket, and read the specifics on food packages at the checkout, count the number of items in the basket of their own or another person, or browse through a newspaper or magazine.

Refocusing is especially useful if you are concerned about physical symptoms or are self-conscious. When we're socially anxious or worried about our physical health, we tend to focus on ourselves – how quickly we breathe, how hot we 're, how much we shake, what pains we have – and this can make us more uncomfortable and anxious even. Refocusing takes away our attention, and this can break the cycle of self-focusing and growing anxiety.

The great thing about refocusing is that it's all around you – you don't need to stress yourself by wondering what you're thinking about – the possibilities are all in view. But not only the things you can see can distract you – what can you hear? What is it you can smell? How does the gravel sound and look when you step over it? How do you like the seat underneath? And the sun shines on your shoulders? You can absorb your thoughts using all of your senses.

Mental exercise

Mental exercise allows you to be imaginative and use more mental energy by putting yourself into a distracting expression, image, or mental activity. A distracting phrase might be a line or two of soothing poetry, and a distracting picture might be the recollection of a beach where you'd feel good, your mental task might be to recite a whole poem, recall in detail a favorite holiday trip, practice mental arithmetic or study someone nearby and try to guess what they're doing, what interests they might have, where they're going, etc. You could try to dwell on an imaginary scene to get your mind away from worrying thoughts; you can distract yourself even more successful by making your scene come alive with color and sounds and texture. Some people enjoy imagining a dream home and then walking through each room, studying the details of the furniture and fittings; some people like to 'hear' a well-loved tune; others are relieved by recalling cycling along with a familiar and loved path, paying attention to the scenery; some people find that they can be absorbed by imagining all the stages involved in making a complex flow. The more complex the mental exercises, the more challenging they are, so it is vital that you work out something that suits you, something that represents your interests and preferences.

General rules guiding distraction

You must select one that suits you and the situation in which you need to be distracted before using the distraction technique. There's no point in dwelling on a sun-soaked beach picture if you hate the sea and sunburn easily, or if you're skiing with your true love. Likewise, relying on physical activity to distract, you won't help if your anxiety attacks occur during interviews. Work out your preferences and needs and then tailor your distraction according to your needs. Try to take advantage of your own interests: if you're a keen gardener, you might use pruning and weed as your physical activity; look through the garden bus window and identify plants as a refocusing exercise, and hold an image of a beautiful formal garden as a mental task.

Be inventive in developing your own selection of distraction techniques when you have determined what you need, but always be specific in your choice of task and choose exercises that require a great deal of attention. Practice them whenever you have a chance when you have a repertoire of distraction techniques for different occasions. This means you can turn your attention to your diversion very quickly when you are stressed.

Now consider when and where to use distraction techniques by recalling the situations you find difficult and then planning which one of your techniques you could use. This list should be as long as you need it to be – aim for more than one or two entries, and remember that there may be more than one distracting solution to a single anxiety-provoking situation.

It's been a very theoretical exercise so far, and you've just considered what's likely to help you – now you have to try your distraction techniques. When you're feeling anxious, put your distraction strategies into action and see what happens. You will find that some of your ideas are going to be successful right from the beginning, which is great, but others will need to be refined. Look back at the less successful experiences and try to understand why a strategy might not have worked for you: maybe the picture you chose did not really reflect your preferences, so it wasn't that engaging; maybe the mental arithmetic you set up was a little too difficult; maybe the setting wasn't right for the physical distraction you chose, and mental distraction would have been too difficult. There can be many reasons why a strategy doesn't work well, and everyone will come across different obstacles; the key is to find out why something didn't work for you at the time. In short, see if your ideas work in real life if they 're not doing the trick altogether, then tinker with them and get them right for you.

Worry and distraction

You might remember that we noted that some of you might be 'worriers' in the introductory sections of this book. If you are, then distraction will be a really useful part of your toolkit for coping. If you can identify your concern (if you can answer the 'What if.'..?' question), then you can first consider whether there is anything you can do about the worry. If so, do it and use problem-solving to help you, but if there's nothing else to do and you're still in increasing anxiety circles, think about the future with lots of 'What if. 'S, then the pattern can be broken by distraction Use distractions to let go of the preoccupations. This will give you relief, but it will also help you to learn that you can stop worrying and that things are going to be OK. You can take responsibility for your worries.

The same applies to the anxiety cycles that are set up when we look back with 'If only.'. 'Reflections (we called that rumination rather than worry). Repeat 'What if you. 'And' If only for... 'Thought increases our distress only, and distraction helps us to disengage and escape the vicious cycles again. Then, we can use our minds to make something more pleasurable or useful.

Difficulties of Distraction

I just don't seem to be able to

It could be you just aren't practiced enough. This is normal and easy to remedy as long as you can find time to rehearse your skills, especially when you're not nervous. The challenge here is finding ways to construct regular practice into your daily life.

When I tried it, it wasn't ideal for me

The technique may not have fitted to the situation. Again, if you have a range of strategies in your toolkit, this is a common problem and easily overcome. Make sure you've considered plenty of different ways to take your mind off worries – go back to your list if necessary and ask friends to help you increase your ideas. Think ahead of time about the anxiety-provoking situation and try to select the best strategy from your toolkit-but also have a back-up idea.

You may already have been too stressed to cope with that. When we are too stressed to cope very well, there comes a point-so always try to catch your anxiety as early as you can. Next time make sure you know your 'early warning signs.' If you are less stressed, any coping technique will work better, but a useful tip is to use the physical activities more when you are highly stressed since they are often easier to put into action than mental activities.

A final and very significant note: Like other people, in coping with worries, concerns, and anxieties, you can find diversion helpful, and it will give you the ability to think and prepare more productively. However, if it is used as a means to escape unpleasant situations, it may be detrimental because it is only used as a protective behavior. For instance, if you were anxious to talk to guests at social gatherings and were always distracted by handing around the drinks, then you would never face your real fear, and it wouldn't go away.

If you use avoidance as a safety technique, or you notice that the concerns keep coming up, then you'll need to learn another mind-control strategy: checking and recalling thoughts and pictures about issues.

Directed Imagery

How many times do you want to run, leave it all behind and head for some warm tropical island or lock yourself away in a snowy hillside log cabin? Not many of us actually have the time to fulfill our deepest wishes, let alone the capital, but you can do the next best thing-directed imagery. This is a technique involving the use of all senses to imagine yourself in a totally comfortable environment. If your mind is there, your body will follow suit and enter a completely relaxed state. Know this can send you to sleep, so don't do it when you need to be somewhere! The best time to do so is in the evening, either before or when you go to bed.

To those with social anxiety disorders, the use of guided imagery for relaxation is a good technique. The sounds of the sea washing up on a sun-kissed Tropical Island, or curled up in front of a huge, roaring log fire while the snow settles outside, are some of the most common things that people imagine or visualize. The aim is to create a scene that will inspire you and not what you're told to imagine. It doesn't really matter what the scene is; what's important is that when you close your eyes, you "experience" every sound, every smell, and every sight, that you transport yourself to that place. Again, if you have a medical condition, you must seek medical advice before doing this.

How to Implement Directed Imagery

For this, we will use the famous beach setting but picture your own personal place of relaxation when you try.

- Find a place, first, quiet and free from distractions
- Take off glasses or contacts and loosen tight clothes
- Rest in a comfortable position and put your hands on your lap or rest on the chair's arms
- Next, take some deep breaths, even directly from your abdomen

- Close your eyes when you feel relaxed and picture the white sandy beach. You lie on this beach, surrounded by sand, swaying palm trees and lapping on the shore of crystal seas.

- The sky above you is cloudless, and you can feel the sun's heat warming your body

- Inhale deeply and smell the tropical flowers and sea salt

- Hear the waves rolling in and the birds chattering around the trees

- Feel the warm, inviting sand beneath your skin and see how fresh a tropical fruit tastes

- Stay there whenever you need to. Notice how much calmer and more relaxed you are and enjoy that feeling as it spreads your own body, from the top of your head to the tips of your fingers and toes.

- Note how distant those feelings of stress and anxiety seem

- Count from 10 backward to 1 when you're ready and slowly open your eyes. You'll feel alert but at the same time totally relaxed

CHAPTER SIX: ASSERTIVENESS – A NECESSARY SKILL IN MANAGING ANXIETY

Assertiveness is another skill that can help you cope with anxiety, fear, and worry. It describes a way to communicate, while still being respectful, your needs, feelings, or rights to others. It is also especially useful when coping with pressures that occur when we have to address something that requires another person – say 'no,' for instance, or return products to a store, or hold one's patience when crossed.

Assertiveness is all about equilibrium: matching the desires and rights with those of others. Contrary to some beliefs, it's not about getting at all costs what you want that's bullying and disrespecting others. But only giving in to other people 's demands may be disrespectful to your needs and freedoms. You might think it's worth it-that by giving in to others it's easier to prevent confrontation-and you might be right. Think of the longer-term implications, too, too. If you don't have a real disadvantage, then OK, but if it means you 're getting put on more and more, or if you end up feeling devalued, or if it just gets harder and harder – to control your kids, for example, or to meet your needs – then you'll probably need to be more assertive.

While some lucky people find it easy to be assertive, others find it challenging – so again, if being assertive is a struggle for you, you are not alone. The reasons for the struggle range from simply not knowing the basic rules of assertiveness or not being confident about your rights to being low in self-esteem and not feeling worthy or having trouble managing anger. Fortunately, not knowing the 'top tips' of assertiveness is easily addressed - in this chapter, we will cover these quickly. We'll also take a good look at your rights and see how you can actually express them.

The theory of assertiveness

Being assertive means, as we have already learned, talking in a way that is straightforward and respectful of ourselves and others. This means not being passive or aggressive or manipulative since none of these approaches shows respect for one another. Manipulation is often expressed as a charming form of aggression, which makes it a powerful form of aggression that can be hard to see as disrespectful. The 'charming' Manipulator is going to cajole and flatter: 'I'm just asking you to do this because you're so smart;' 'I'm just talking about what's good for you when I say 'no.' It's easy to be hoodwinked into assuming you don't get bullied. Assertiveness sits somewhere between passivity and manipulation or aggression.

Becoming Assertive

Very obviously, we don't respect ourselves if we are passive, and if we are violent or deceptive, we don't value others. The goal of being assertive is to achieve a particular type of interaction that does not undermine either party and involves balance. Being passive is not balanced because, in the process, it means avoiding conflict but disrespecting oneself. Being aggressive or manipulative tips the balance in the other direction-the objective here is to win, regardless of the rights of the other person.

The Passive Person tends to refrain from conflict, can't make decisions, and always aims to please others. If this is you, then you may well feel very frustrated as you don't get your needs met, and you may even start feeling resentful and devalued – neither of which is good for your self-esteem or stress levels.

The Openly Aggressive Type can seem forceful, even bullying, ignoring other people's rights and needs in the quest to win. If you want to be violent, in the short term, you can get what you want, but you need to ask yourself if the strategy works for you in the longer term. Can you survive relationships? Do you feel good about yourself? The aggressive attack by the Manipulator is cleverly covered up. This person may seem considerate but will use emotional blackmail in the form of charm, or they might say things aimed at undermining the other person's confidence. They are not fighting fair. Again, if you tend to take a manipulative stance, ask yourself if it will work well for you in the long term or if you find that you are losing friends and others' trust and respect.

The Assertive Individual takes a broad view of the situation and considers both sides of the argument in such a way that they can make a strong case for what is rational. The goal is to say simply and politely what they want: quite a different image from the passive and aggressive forms.

Once you've got a good argument, you must deliver it in the best possible way. Just by attending to your body language and choosing words, you can send out the message that when you make your request, you are not timid or hostile. To make this easier, here are some tips to get your presentation to the fullest:

- Facial expression: try to express yourself in a firm, friendly way. Avoid an aggressive, tense look or one that suggests you 're nervous.

- Posture: keep the head up (but not so high that it looks haughty!) – lowering it will make you look submissive.

- Distance: not too near but near enough to make good eye contact and to be noticed.

- Gestures: make them comfortable and not threatening – for starters, no finger-wagging. But make sure you don't make nervous gestures like wringing your hands, too.

- Eye contact: don't glare at anyone else, but don't be afraid to look them in the eye. During a conversation, a comfortable pattern is to change your focus between the other person's eyes and mouth.

- Voice: keep your voice tone, volume, and pace so that it communicates calmness and thoughtfulness. Seek not to let your voice pitch or volume go up, which we feel anxious can easily do.

- Vocabulary: use terms and phrases that are positive and non-critical-the aim is to get the other person on board, not conflict. Recognize the other side of the argument, feel empathetic, and never attack.

Perhaps the biggest 'top tip' is on Keep Calm. This is always more easily said than achieved, as you may know, but by now, you have a clear understanding of stress-management techniques and maybe have adapted them to suit you. Nevertheless, a brief reminder of the main aspects of maintaining calm is given below:

- Be prepared: if you can, get your case backed up by the facts and rehearse what you want to say. Try out a friend's statement and get some feedback

- Be aware of your feelings and try to 'resist' them- don't ignore them

- Catch nervousness and anger as soon as possible – it's easier to deal with them earlier than later, and by now you've probably got a good set of skills to manage the unhelpful feelings

- Have a 'mantra' to help you stay calm

- Use physical relaxation and calm, regular respiration techniques

- Occupy yourself where needed

- Keep to the point: Don't be side-tracked and repeat as often as you need

Forgive the repetition, but it's such an important point that it's worth saying again: the goal of being assertive is not to win at all costs, but to arrive at a reasonable all-round solution. Therefore, this can involve negotiation and compromise. Your strongest position is one where you've already thought how far you'd be willing to compromise – so:

- Decide, beforehand, how far you will compromise
- Set boundaries and be prepared to stick to them until the talks change your mind sincerely
- If you stand on your ground, accept that it will have consequences; the other person may be uncooperative or even aggressive – but in Step 3 we will look at ways to deal with this

Those compromises may look like this in the examples above:

- To be prepared to wait until the next tax year for a new computer when the department will have a new budget – but not to wait any longer than this.

- To allow the kids to keep toys out in their own rooms and to help the kids put away toys in the living room when they're particularly tired – but to keep the responsibility on them.

- On the day of the transfer, to be available by text to provide advice if appropriate.

Step 3: Ready to refuse manipulation

You are all eventually set to be assertive. If you've prepared well, and feel confident, there's a good chance you'll be heard. You also need to be prepared for the other person not to 'play the ball'-not respectfully listening to you. If the other person simply refuses your request or refuses to accept your argument, then you can remain calm, knowing you've been thinking through the consequences – you 're going to go to a higher authority, you 're going to stop making phone calls, etc. It's a shame you 're now being pushed to do this, but it's better than just giving in.

The 'manipulators' who will be using charm or bullying to get their way are harder to deal with. They 're going to try to make you feel flattered or guilty, to undermine you. But how do we learn they exploit us? A telltale sign feels bad when it comes to making our request.

Imagine you 'd claimed your boss gave you too much work to do. You had thought through this and discussed it with a friend, and although you recognized the department was very busy, you still felt unreasonably burdened, and your request for less work was fair. Instead of respecting your statement and considering your point of view, your boss reacts by using manipulative criticism aimed at making you feel guilty or simply stupid. Your boss could be using tricks like:

Nagging: 'Don't you mind, didn't you finish it yet? Your problem is you're too slow. Now get the job done.'

Reading: 'Well, the real problem is obviously that you don't organize yourself well enough and what you should do is.

Insults: 'Typical woman: is unable to cope with the real world.'

Hurt: 'You made me feel awful...

Your manager may be more subtle than this and use deceptive 'concern' to make you feel appreciated and thankful that your request or point of view is not being considered. This is a more powerful strategy because we can feel good about the situation initially, and we do not realize that we were manipulated. Reality could hit us later. If your boss used to make a false concern, you might hear:

If you know you need to be assertive, thorough training is your best starting point: practice your assertive statement and practice yourself. You will be able to be more 'spontaneous' with practice, but you will have to invest in preparation time in the early days. There are four following steps:

Phase 1: Decide what you want.. (and ensure it's reasonable)

Put yourself at the center and ask: What am I going to want? That sounds so obvious, but if you're used to putting others first, simply considering your needs can be quite difficult. So forget everyone else for a moment and think about your wishes and then clearly state them. For example, you might want a new work computer ('I want a new work computer'); you might want your kids to clean up their toys every night ('I want you to put away your toys before you go to bed'); you might want to say no to your friend's offer to help her move home ('I can't help you move home next week'). You should also think about how you feel about the current situation, as this may be relevant to your discussion. Do you feel hurt, disgusted, and frustrated?

Now it's time to remember someone else's viewpoint. Balance your wishes with other people's needs and rights by asking yourself: Am I sensible? If you tend towards the aggressive or manipulative end of the spectrum, this is more of a challenge, but try to put yourself in the shoes of the other person and see things from their perspective. A balanced argument will be more engaging than an aggressive one, and remember that your objective is not to win at all costs, but to put forward a sensible and considerate proposal. You might infer that when you have thought things through:

- Requesting a new computer is reasonable, as other members of your team have more up-to-date models, although you might be aware that the department's money is tight

- It's reasonable to ask your kids to clean up before bed because your home is pretty small and the living room is easily cluttered, and they need to learn how to clean themselves up – but you might also think they can have more freedom in their own bedrooms.

- Refusing your friend's request is reasonable, as she has given you little notice and you already have other commitments

Then think about your point and try to express the implications of the cooperation of the other person. There might be constructive – 'It will help me do my work much more effectively and not waste time due to computer failures;' 'If you tidy up each evening for a week, I'll send you extra pocket money' – or simply practical – 'If you feel you can't approve a new machine, then I will go to the Head Office of the Region and make the request there' – or there could be a negative message ' Overall, positive outcomes are more successful – reward works better than punishment – and, for example, praising the children for good behavior is safer in the long run than punishing them for undesirable behaviors.

Step 2: State your wishes

Now you have the foundation for an assertive statement: you know what you want, you think it's reasonable, and you've been thinking through the consequences. It's time to rehearse what you're going to say, and if you follow these rules you can make your argument more effective:

Be positive and intelligent

Be fair – do not make personal attacks

State the implications

Have a brief look

"I need a new PC. My old one is unreliable, and although I appreciate we don't have a generous budget anymore, I need a new computer to do my job properly. I'll be very grateful if you can do this, but if you can't authorize it, I'll be making the request through Head Office."

"Dad and I are really happy with the way you look after your toys, and now we want you to tidy them up in the living room before you go to bed. I don't mind if you have any toys lying around in your own bedrooms, but the living room is for all of us, and at the end of the day, I want it clean. If you do this, Dad and I will be very pleased, and at the end of the week, we'll be giving you a little more pocket money."

"I would normally be more than happy to help, especially since I appreciate that moving is a huge stress for you, but this time, I can't be there. I have dedicated myself to next week already. I can spend an hour or two during the weekend helping you pack, but I can't help with the move itself."

You can see that none of these statements are complicated or long, but all of them are polite, and all of them start quite positively. That is what a good argument is all about. A good argument puts the other person on board, hiring them, so they listen to you. If you are critical or negative, then there is a risk that you will lose your attention and any hope of cooperation.

- Caring: 'That is all well indeed, however, I truly feel that it is to your greatest advantage to improve your aptitudes via conveying a generous outstanding task at hand.'
- Concern: 'On the off chance that you are having these issues, would you say you are certain you're directly for this activity, all things considered?'

Advice: 'Let me mention to you what I would do in the event that I was you. .'

Every one of these reactions is proposed to side-line your necessities and your privileges and to avoid your contention. To manage this, you should build up the aptitudes and certainty to hold fast. There are two especially valuable ways to deal with the assistance you to be progressively self-assured and handle manipulative analysis and bogus 'concern':

1. the 'broken record.'

2. getting ready for analysis

It is additionally valuable to revive your attention to your fundamental social rights. A few of us – especially the more latent – will, in general, think little of our privileges, and this can hinder being genuinely decisive. Recollect that we each have the accompanying rights:

- To be dealt with deferentially (it is most significant that you recall this)

- To state what we need and express an assessment (deferentially, obviously)

- To commit errors (sensibly speaking)

- To alter our perspectives when we have surveyed a circumstance

- To not know/get something and to request more data

- To request an explanation of contention, so we recognize what we are managing

- To take the time that you need – you can say, 'let me consider this,' or, 'i'll hit you up on this,' or, 'i can't settle on a choice at the present time, i will need to give it more idea.'

Something different that will help is advising yourself that you have given a ton of Thought to your contention, and you realize that it is reasonable – and you could generally look at this with a companion in the event that you are in question. When you are sure that your announcement is sensible, at that point, stick to it, utilizing the procedure called the 'broken record.'

The 'broken record.'

This procedure is appropriately named in light of the fact that you essentially continue rehashing your contention. On the off chance that we are unassertive, we take 'No' for an answer extremely effectively, and we are not tireless in coming to a meaningful conclusion. Essential decisiveness expertise is being industrious and rehashing what you need – smoothly. Keep in mind, you have concluded that you are offering a reasonable and sensible expression, so feel free to declare it. Notwithstanding absurd restriction (that is, the point at which the other individual isn't tuning in to your contention), essentially rehash your message. Frequently you will find that the other individual starts to tune in.

This is an especially valuable methodology when your privileges are plainly at risk for being mishandled, or when you are probably going to be redirected by articulate yet unessential contentions, or when you feel helpless in light of the fact that you realize the other individual will utilize analysis to sabotage your confidence. Interestingly, when you have arranged your 'content,' you can unwind and rehash your contention, realizing that you are being sensible and comprehending what you are going to state. This implies you are considerably less prone to be derailed, injurious, or manipulative the other individual attempts to be.

Plainly it can get dreary on the off chance that you use the very same explanation again and again without variety, so you can marginally fluctuate the manner in which you express it each time. In the model beneath, you will perceive how it is conceivable to hold fast despite forceful control that is expected to initiate blame and self-question.

As a rule, the individual you are managing will begin to tune in to your contention. Be that as it may, a few people may play dreadful and utilize inside and out affront to attempt to control you, and if there is a trace of legitimacy in the reactions, you can wind up wrong-footed by this. This is the point of the controller; in such a case that they can occupy you away from your contention, they have a superior potential for success of subverting your endeavors. Along these lines, ensure that you have set yourself up for managing analysis.

Getting ready for analysis

You can 'stress-evidence' yourself gigantically by being set up for analysis. On the off chance that you are not readied, at that point, manipulative analysis may leave you feeling so awful about yourself that you consent to accomplish something you would prefer not to do. Analysis that gets to us frequently holds a trace of validity – that is, the reason it very well may be so successful – yet it is misrepresented. For instance, a supervisor may state: That's run of the mill of you – you're continually requesting, nothing is ever sufficient!

The facts might confirm that an individual has exclusive expectations and has requested things previously, yet saying that he is 'continually' requesting and that 'nothing is ever' sufficient may be a barefaced embellishment. Once more, the facts might demonstrate that an individual is pondering her own needs at the present time, yet this doesn't imply that she is 'narrow-minded'; she may have thought about what is reasonable, and this analysis is overstated.

Be that as it may, on the off chance that we are not readied, these sorts of manipulative remarks can so effectively trigger blame – and afterward, we yield.

The essential thing isn't to draw in with the analysis – let it wash over you and return to your contention. This is such a great amount of simpler to do on the off chance that you've considered ahead time exactly what may be tossed at you. On the off chance that the man in the primary model knows that he has exclusive expectations, or the lady in the subsequent model knows that she is requesting something for herself, at that point, they won't be shocked when the reactions are tossed at them. They will, at that point have the option to handle the analysis tranquility by recognizing that there might be a trace of validity in it, before coming back to their contention. For instance:

CHAPTER SEVEN: MANAGING ANXIETY WITH HEALTHY NUTRITION

How many times have you heard the saying, "You are what you eat?" This is valid to some degree. You are eating healthy food, and you are becoming healthy. You eat garbage, and your body turns into garbage. You eat foods that help you stay calm and calm down. Eating the right foods can greatly improve your ability to manage well and cope well with anxiety. The right to eat includes whole foods, herbs, and supplements.

Whole Foods You can Enjoy

Eating whole food is always healthier, no matter how you put it than eating processed foods, no matter how healthy the manufacturers claim to be their foods. A great guiding principle to assess how healthy – or unhealthy – a food item is: the Principle of Paleo. The theory states that the closer it is to the original type of a food item, the better it is. So between a piece of apple and a slice of apple pie, it's clear who's healthier among the two.

Why is the food processed less than whole ones? With too much packaging, like frying, much of the food's important and beneficial nutrients get lost. Worse, some processing methods actually make food unhealthy either by changing the molecular structure of the food or by adding unhealthy ingredients. And if you want to be able to handle and cope very well with your social anxiety, you will need all the nutrients you can get and minimize unhealthy ingredients too.

The Mayo Clinic promotes several dietary practices as regards coping with and managing social anxiety, or just about any anxiety disorder. One such is eating a high-protein breakfast. This is because protein eating makes you feel full for longer periods of time. It also helps you stabilize your blood sugar levels the rest of the morning for stable energy.

The Mayo Clinic encourages going for another dietary regimen for complex carbohydrates, instead of basic ones. Carbohydrates can help you manage your social anxiety, as it increases serotonin production in your brain. As you have learned earlier, higher serotonin levels are beneficial to anxiety, as they help calm you down. Why difficult carbs? It's because complex carbs help you maintain a stable level of blood sugar, which not only makes you more vigorous and alert but also lowers your risk of diabetes. Those are two less worrisome things.

Another good dietary habit the Mayo Clinic is advocating to cope with, and control anxiety is to drink enough water every day. Dehydration can affect your mood in ways that can worsen your anxiety. Go for 6 to 8 glasses a day as a general rule, and don't wait until your urine turns dark yellow in color before going for a gulp. You're already dehydrated by this time. Unlike all other nutrition experts, the Mayo Clinic also advocates for regular, nutritious meals to eat, which is also vital for optimal mental wellbeing. Load up, in particular, on fresh fruits and vegetables, and omega-3 fatty acids, which are abundant in fish such as salmon and trout. Only keep in mind that even though you consume safe and nutritious meals, be careful not to over-feed.

Some of the best whole foods to eat to manage and cope with your social anxiety – or any general anxiety disorder – include:

- Acai Berries: As with blueberries, this is another superfood packed with antioxidants and phytonutrients.
- Almonds: The high zinc content of this nut is one strong reason to go nuts. Zinc plays an important role in keeping a

mood balanced, which helps to reduce anxiety. It's also iron-rich, which is important because anemia can make your anxiety worse by making you feel more tired than usual.

- Blueberries: This nutritionally rich super-food contains a lot of phytonutrients, antioxidants, and vitamins, which can help combat stress.

- Hallelujah, chocolates! Yes, you read that correctly! Keep your horses though, and I'm not thinking about those commercial versions that are heavily refined and sugar-filled like Cadbury, Snickers, and Hershey. I refer to sugar and milk-free dark chocolate – the purest kind. Pure dark chocolates contain compounds that boost mood. It helps to bring down levels of cortisol, too. Recall cortisol-a secretion of stress?

- Seaweeds: A great alternative with whole grains to get enough Magnesium and tryptophan.

- Whole Grains: This can be a great help to you, but only if you're not gluten prone. Whole grains are loaded with Magnesium (not getting enough of which can exacerbate anxiety), complex carbs for steady energy, and tryptophan for the calming hormone serotonin production.

Herbs

Did you know that herbs can also help you with your social anxiety, besides making many of your dishes even more delicious? One of the reasons is that they are all-natural and are therefore healthy. Second, some herbs have properties that can help in managing anxiety. Those herbs are:

- Lavender: Oil extracted from this herb was found to be as effective in managing persistent generalized anxiety disorder as known as anti-anxiety Benzie – Lorazepam – in a 2010 study. The nice part, right? This has not got the same sedative effects. How to put it to use? Start with aromatherapy of 80 milligrams per day for relief from anxiety.

- Passionflower: According to the University of Maryland Medical Center, studies have shown that this herb works just as well as certain Benzies to cope with and manage anxiety but – as with lavender – with less sedation. In another study, it has also been shown that it helps to reduce anxiety, agitation, irritability, and depression in recovering former opium addicts. How to put it to use? Start with 90 milligrams of its liquid extract or three times a day with a cup of passionflower tea.

- Lemon balm: Commonly used with other plants, this plant can also help control and cope with anxiety by itself. A published study was conducted in 2004, which showed lemon balm (600 milligrams to be exact), which made the participants of the study more alert and calmer, as well as decreasing their stress levels. How does one use it? Start by drinking one teaspoon dried lemon balm tea up to four times a day.

- Chamomile Tea: This is a tea that does not stimulate you to become more alert but helps you to calm down, making it much easier for you to cope with and manage your social anxiety. It contains beneficial compounds that mimic the effect of another Benzie, Valium, which binds to important receptors in your brain. In fact, a study by the University of Pennsylvania revealed that anxiety symptoms of subjects decreased significantly after taking chamomile tea for eight weeks.

- Hops: Sorry, this refers not to the finished product (beer) but to the ingredients themselves. Hop extracts can be used in particular for aromatherapy n your pillows buy stuffing them with it. Because of its bitter taste, it is rarely drunk as tea.

Healthy Supplements

It is virtually impossible nowadays to get all of your daily nutrition requirements from food alone. It's because most agricultural soils are already tired these days, i.e., because of over-farming, significantly reduced nutritional content. In reality, the people of ages ago, in terms of understanding soil fatigue, seemed wiser than us. The old testament of the Bible mandated the Jewish people to let their agricultural soil rest after every seven years for one year, by not planting anything on them.

Another reason not to be able to get all of our nutritional requirements from whole foods – especially veggies and fruits – is the long-distance storage and transportation. Long storage periods tend to remove minerals and vitamins from most of the foods, especially the Vitamin B-complex and C.

Lastly, heating food also results in the destruction of nutrients, especially cooking at high heat. Since it is unpalatable for most people to eat raw foods that are not called sushi and sashimi, it is highly unlikely that all nutrients can be obtained from eating whole raw food.

Would you like to know how impossible it is to get all the essential vitamins and minerals you recommend daily allowance (RDA) for? Consider vitamin E, roughly 30 IU or international units of which are RDA. To get this much from your daily meal, you'll need to eat:

- 10 pounds, or 40 ears of fresh corn on average;

- 2 kilograms of the wheat germ;

- Three livres of almonds;

- 33 Lbs of spinach, or

- 50 Lb Broccoli.

Considering the impossibility of eating that much food in a single day, also consider the fact that this is only for vitamin E alone. And all the other important minerals and vitamins? As early as now, I can tell you that if you tried this, your tummy would explode!

Now that I have argued for supplements, here are a few supplements that can help you cope well with and manage your social anxiety:

- Gamma-Amino Butyric Acid: Also known for brevity as GABA, there is some evidence for its ability to help improve relaxation. As such, it is thought to help in managing symptoms of anxiety.

- Kava: This anxiety management supplement is the most common and popular in the market. It is possibly also the one with the most scientific support. Studies also have shown that with some of the more common anxiety prescription drugs on the market, it can stand toe-to-toe. Even as a supplement, it is similar to prescription medicines because it does not mix well with alcohol, along with other prescription medicines. Also, if you have a history of liver disease or an alcoholic, either recovering or still one, you might do well to avoid this. But even if you're in the clear, and this isn't pharmaceutical grade stuff, you would do well to get clearance from your doctor first.

- Magnesium: It is widely believed that not getting enough Magnesium can lead to or exacerbate symptoms of anxiety, such as panic disorder or social anxiety. Magnesium is an essential mineral for healthy nerves, which can affect levels of anxiety.

- Melatonin: The supplementary source of this sleep-inducing hormone that exists naturally in your body is considered to be an anxiety reduction help with strong potential. It's because it will help alleviate some of your tension because it's a calming effect on your body. Take care though, in some places, melatonin needs to be administered, so make sure you have one if you're in a position it's required. It can also cause you to fall asleep against your wishes, especially at higher dosages. As such, make sure that you start measuring tolerance by half of the smallest dosage possible.

- Passionflower: This herb can also be obtained in dietary supplement form. Though not as powerful as Kava, it does not react to alcohol and is still generally beneficial in managing levels of anxiety.

- Valerian Root: The form of this herb-inducing sleep supplement can help you relax, which is good for managing your social anxiety. Indeed, several studies have confirmed its potential to help boost anxiety-related symptoms.

- Vitamin B12: This vitamin is essential to a healthy nervous system, as is Magnesium. Some studies have also shown that vitamin B12 supplementing the diet will help boost anxiety symptoms.

Precaution guiding the use of supplements

Despite not being regarded as medicinal and thus not having any prescriptions, you should do well to contact the doctor first before taking such supplements. Better safe than sorry because these can impede your ability to work, study, or do other important things, especially if you have a medical condition or are taking other prescription medicines or supplements. Prevention is always better than cure.

How to Build a Diet against Anxiety

We can't blame food for anxiety, but what you eat and how you eat is a part of how you cope with anxiety. Some foods are "made" to produce anxiety symptoms, while others may be able to help you battle those symptoms.

The reality is that diet really matters because it's a loop of viciousness. Many people who feel anxious are going to eat comfort foods, so they feel better. But the food you eat has a direct effect on the way you 're feeling, and the levels of anxiety you 're feeling – high sugar, high carb foods make you feel better, but only for a short while, while other foods release certain good chemicals. Getting the right balance can be a very valuable instrument to help you cope with the symptoms of a social anxiety disorder.

We've all used the word "eating healthy," it's one that's tossed a little around these days, but eating a balanced diet really makes a difference when it comes to anxiety. Filling your plate with vegetables will counter the symptoms of anxiety much better than a plate full of unhealthy burgers. The way to create an anti-anxiety diet is to remove some foods that might very well contribute to your symptoms of anxiety. The following foods should be taken away, or at least moderated:

- **Fried foods**-they is extremely difficult to digest; they contain very little nutrition and also contribute to the risk of heart disease. If your body can't handle the food you consume properly, you'll fail to overcome the symptoms of anxiety

- **Alcohol-**Many people with an anxiety disorder turn to alcohol in the mistaken belief that everything will improve. It is not. Besides the fact that too much can make you do stupid things, alcohol does not make any favors for your body. It is dehydrated, throws off your hormones, and even wipes out your nutrient balance. And the toxins that get into your body can cause symptoms of physical anxiety.

- **Coffee**-Caffeine is a stimulant and will not cause any anxiety symptoms in moderation. The more you consume this, however, the worse your risk becomes. Coffee also makes your heart beat faster as well as other sensations, which can lead to panic attacks. Limit the intake to one cup a day.

- **Non-Dairy products** are not harmful to you, as long as you eat them in moderation. Large amounts of milk can cause your levels of adrenaline to rise, and that can contribute to increased anxiety. Reduce the amount you eat, and if you think drinking milk causes your symptoms to worsen, cut back or cut it out entirely.

- **Refined Sugar**-While, the fruit sugar is not bad; the dessert sugar is good. Similar to caffeine, sugar stimulates the human body to produce a certain shakiness, which can help to exacerbate any of your symptoms of anxiety.

- **Foods That Produce Acid**-Milk, cheese, pickles, wine, sour cream, and liver all generate acid in the body, and there is a strong reason to assume that such foods often decrease the magnesium levels in the body. Low Magnesium is one of the contributors to or causes of anxiety, particularly in those who already have an anxiety disorder, so cutting back or out these foods altogether is a wise choice.

While avoiding these types of food will not cure you of your anxiety disorder, it can certainly help, particularly if you find you eat too much of one or more of them. You don't have to consume a diet of rabbit foods; most of the foods can still be consumed, but consistency is the key here if you want to help you minimize symptoms of anxiety. Remember this – a nutritionally sound body is more able to fight off the symptoms than one filled with junk foods.

6 Foods which help you to combat anxiety

So, you know the foods to avoid, but are you sure about which foods to eat? The following foods will help in my anxiety symptoms. Eating a healthy diet helps your hormones function properly, leading to a sense of wellbeing at large. Try to take these foods into your diet:

- **Fresh fruit** – Your body needs a certain amount of sugar and carbohydrates, but the refined ones are not necessary. Fresh fruit contains natural sugars that are burned off and converted into energy. They also contain essential nutrients, including vitamins and antioxidants. Blueberries and peaches are the top two.

- **Vegetables**-In particular, if you have an anxiety disorder, vegetables are much more important than fruits. Most vegetables contain high levels of fiber and are packed full of vitamins, especially in those with anxiety disorders, which are rapidly depleted.

- **Water**-The majority of people get dehydrated if they don't drink enough water anywhere. Dehydration keeps the body in an anxious state, and this can make fighting off the symptoms even harder. Aim to consume at least 1 1/2 to 2 liters of water a day.

- **Foods Rich in Tryptophan**-Such foods has proven highly effective in helping to alleviate anxiety symptoms. They include a component that naturally helps you relax and can also help you increase your metabolism, which is always a bonus. Includes poultry, soy, sesame seeds, and oats.

- **Foods that are rich in Magnesium** – about 25 % of the population is deficient in Magnesium, and that's one of the nutrients that play a major role in the human body, Magnesium is involved in more than 300 different processes in the body, and it's crucial that you get enough. Feedingstuffs such as tofu and black beans are rich in Magnesium.

- **Omega-3 Fatty Acids** – While omega-3 fatty acid research is still ongoing, we do know that this is a vital nutrient for anxiety and depression. You can get fatty fish omega 3's, such as salmon and mackerel, winter squash, and flaxseed.

CONCLUSION

At the end of the day, anxiety is not a single situation, but how you respond to it. This can be triggered by something and everything, and because it comes from your own belief systems, it can be difficult to manage it. However, that is not impossible.

The first thing that you can do is accept your anxieties. Know you 're nervous and feel a lack of control; it's going to go a long way to help you overcome that. If you don't admit there is a problem, you can't start fighting it anyway! Make it simpler by trying to think positively about yourself. Do not take it too seriously – have fun and take a more relaxed approach to things so that the little stuff doesn't get stressed out.

Be mindful of what makes you distress and then address the problem in a calm way, rationally. Don't be afraid to ask if you need help! The main aim of therapists is to make your life easier-contact them, and they will certainly set you on the right path.

Also, in a day or two, anxiety won't disappear and leave you with a 'live happily ever after'! More often than not, life tends to be a struggle. You may or may not be cured of your anxiety by practicing these techniques, but they will definitely help you get a better handle. You'll find you 're able to work with it, and even though it when you need to combat it all the time instead. Practice these techniques regularly and do not give up if you do not immediately see effects. Be patient and be vigilant, and you'll find yourself getting better and better every day before long!

Now that you know these tips, the next step is to keep practicing them. You may want to pick up this book, again and again, to read through some specific chapters just to remind yourself of how powerful you are against anxiety. Yes, you can live your best life, anxiety-free, and that time is NOW!

Once again, thank you for picking this book! I hope that has given you a meaningful start to manage your anxiety and take control of your life!

CPSIA information can be obtained
at www.ICGtesting.com
Printed in the USA
BVHW061004040321
601713BV00012B/1121

9 781801 918428